THE TRICK

T0353535

Eve Leigh

THE TRICK

OBERON BOOKS
LONDON

WWW.OBERONBOOKS.COM

First published in 2019 by Oberon Books Ltd
521 Caledonian Road, London N7 9RH
Tel: +44 (0) 20 7607 3637 / Fax: +44 (0) 20 7607 3629
e-mail: info@oberonbooks.com
www.oberonbooks.com

A catalogue record for this book is available from the British Library.

PB ISBN: 9781786827326
E ISBN: 9781786827302

eBook conversion by Lapiz Digital Services, India.

Cover design by Studio Doug; Photography by Bronwen Sharp

10 9 8 7 6 5 4 3 2 1

For my mother.

The Trick, produced by HighTide and Loose Tongue, in association with Bush Theatre, premiered at Bush Theatre on 19 February 2019 ahead of touring.

Cast:
1 Lachele Carl
2 Ani Nelson
3 Sharlene Whyte
4 David Verrey

Creative Team:

Director	Roy Alexander Weise
Set & Costume Designer	Jemima Robinson
Lighting Designer	Amy Mae
Sound Designer	Odinn Orn Hilmarsson
Movement Director	Jenni Jackson
Assistant Director	Thomas Bailey
Stage Manager	Julia Nimmo
Production Manager	Steve Watling

Production Sponsors	Lansons
	Harold Hyam Wingate Foundation
	The Sylvia Waddilove Foundation UK

Special thanks to Tom, Mama, and David; Pippa Hill, Réjane Collard-Walker, Erica Whyman, and everyone at the RSC; Roy Alexander Weise; Matt Maltby, David Ralf, and everyone at Loose Tongue; Steven Atkinson, Francesca Clark, Robyn Keynes, Holly White, and everyone at HighTide; Stewart Pringle; the entire astonishing team at the Bush Theatre; Alison, Keith, Sam, and Charlie Penn, in whose front room most of this play was written; Stage One; Arts Council England; Angela Winter, Clare-Hope Ashitey, T'Nia Miller, and Richard Derrington; Jessica Stewart; and Daisaku Ikeda, for everything.

CAST AND CREATIVE TEAM

Lachele Carl (1)
Lachele was born in Pittsburgh, Pennsylvania, and graduated with a degree in Theatre from Point Park College. She lives and works in the UK.
Her theatre credits include: *A Streetcar Named Desire* (Young Vic), *Gods and Monsters* (Southwark Playhouse), Theatre Festival (Theatre 503), *Albans Gardens, The Notebook of Trigorin* (Finborough), and with The Chronic Love Dispensary, *Life Mater* and *Penetration.*
Television credits include: *Doctor Who, Torchwood, The Sarah Jane Mysteries, Ambassadors, The Honourable Woman, Modus 2, Holby City, Deep State* and *Into The Badlands.*
Film credits include: *Denial, Showdogs.*

Ani Nelson (2)
Ani trained at the Academy of Live and Recorded Arts (ALRA).
Her theatre credits include *Abigail's Party* (Hull Truck Theatre), *A Cratchit Christmas* (Theatre 503), *Underwater Love* (Futures Theatre), *The Revenger's Tragedy* (Rose Theatre Bankside), *Game* (Courtyard Theatre).
Television credits include: *Roadkill* (Channel 4).
Film credit include: *Crooked House* (Brilliant Films).

Sharlene Whyte (3)
Sharlene trained at RADA.
Her theatre credits include: *Matilda the Musical* (Cambridge Theatre), *As Good a Time As Any* (Print Room), *Wildefire* (Hampstead Theatre), *Nut* (National Theatre), *Treasure Island* (Theatre Royal, Haymarket), *Julius Caesar* (Lyric Hammersmith), *Born Bad* (Hampstead), *The Three Birds* (Gate), *Arabian Nights* (Young Vic/ tour).
Television credits include: *Home Alone 2, Casualty, Critical, Jonathan Creek: The Case of the Savant's Thumb, Sadie J, Truckers, Run, Mightier Than the Sword, Spooks, The Undisclosed, Coronation Street, Doctors, Waterloo Road, Silent Witness, The Story of Tracy Beaker, Tinsel Town, My Hero, Burnside, As If, Other People's Children.*
Film credits include: *Second Coming, Video, Second Nature, High Heels and Low Lifes.*

David Verrey (4)

Theatre credits include: *Losing Venice* (Orange Tree), *Platonov, Ivanov* (Chichester Festival Theatre and National Theatre), *One Man Two Guvnors, The Recruiting Officer, The Madness of George III, The Coast of Utopia, England People Very Nice* (National Theatre), *Mirror Teeth* (Finborough), *The Years Between* (Northampton), *The Charming Man* (Theatre503), *Romeo and Juliet, A Midsummer Night's Dream* (ESC), *Laughter on the 23rd Floor, Drums in the Night, Filumena* (Manchester Library), *Dead, Falstaff!, Dawn Made Myth, The 1985 Show, Shrivings* (Edinburgh Festival), *Accidental Death of an Anarchist* (Contact), *The Comedy of Errors* (RSC), *The Tempest* (Rose), *The White Devil* (Pentameters), *The Merchant of Venice, Fiddler on the Roof, And Then There Were None* (Wolsey, Ipswich), *Measure for Measure, Macbeth* (Theatre Unlimited), *Lock Up Your Daughters* (Belgrade, Coventry), *A Midsummer Night's Dream* (New End).

Television credits include: *The Long Song, Doctors, Holby City, The Game, Doctor Who, Ripper Street, Garrow's Law, Little Dorrit, Game of Thrones, Judge John Deed, Casanova, The Art of the Garden, Red Dwarf, Birds of a Feather, Law and Order UK, Future Tense: The Story Of H.G. Wells, Poirot, The Fear, Diamond Geezer II, Ultimate Force, Family Affairs, Paul Merton: The Series, The Bill, London's Burning, Kavanagh QC, Pieces of a Silver Lining, Masterworks, Dream Team, Knightmare, Lexx, Supply and Demand, The Musketeers.*

Film credits include: *The Secret Garden, The Terrible Tale of Henrietta Tate, Bridget Jones: Edge of Reason, Attack on Leningrad, Sixty-Six, Magwitch, Secret Weapon.*

Eve Leigh (**Writer**)

Eve is a playwright and theatre-maker. She was the recipient of the 2017 Royal Court commission for the Royal Welsh College of Music and Drama, with her play, *Spooky Action at a Distance*, produced by the Royal Court, RWCMD, and Gate Theatre. She was the first artist-in-residence at the Experimental Stage of the National Theatre of Greece. Her plays *Silent Planet* and *Stone Face* were produced by the Finborough Theatre and published by Oberon Books. *Stone Face* was shortlisted for three Offies, including Best New Play. Other plays include *The Curtain* (Young Vic Taking Part), *Plunder* (Young Vic Taking Part), *Red Sky at Night* (Bush Theatre), *Rapture* (Soho Theatre), *Enough* (Birmingham REP Young Rep). Eve was dramaturg on *How to Win Against History* (Young Vic). Upcoming commissions include work for the Bush Theatre, the Royal Shakespeare Company, The Place/DanceEast, 36 МАЙМУНИ (Sofia), and DOCK11 (Berlin).

Roy Alexander Weise (Director)
Roy is the 19th annual winner of the James Menzies-Kitchin Award and directed his critically-acclaimed, sell-out production of *The Mountaintop* by Katori Hall at the Young Vic. He was shortlisted for the Evening Standard Emerging Talent Award 2018. Theatre credits include: *Nine Night* (National Theatre, and currently running at the Trafalgar Studios), *Br'er Cotton* (Theatre 503, Winner of Best New Play at the Offie Awards), *Heretic Voices* (Arcola Theatre), *Jekyll and Hyde* (National Youth Theatre), *Dead Don't Floss* (National Theatre), *The Ugly One* (Park Theatre, Buckland Theatre Company), *The Dark* (Fuel & Ovalhouse), *Zero For The Young Dudes* (Young & Talented in association with NT Connections), *Primetime* (Royal Court) and *Stone Face* (Finborough Theatre). Assistant Director credits include: *Hangmen* (Royal Court and West End), *X, Escaped Alone, You For Me For You, Primetime 2015, Violence and Son, Who Cares, Liberian Girl* (Royal Court), *Albion, We Are Proud To Present...* (Bush Theatre) and *The Serpent's Tooth* (Talawa/ Almeida Theatre). For Television, Roy was Trainee Director on *Invisible* (Red Room/Ballet Boys/Channel 4). Roy has previously worked at the Royal Court as the Trainee Director, at the Bush Theatre and Lyric Hammersmith as the BBC Theatre Fellow and at The Red Room as Associate Artist. Roy is now Associate Director at the Harts Theatre Company and Lead Acting Tutor at Young & Talented School of Stage & Screen.

Jemima Robinson (Set & Costume Designer)
Jemima was awarded the Max Rayne Design Bursary at the National Theatre which she completed in March 2018. She is a winner of the biennial Linbury Prize for Stage Design and has been nominated for Best Set Design at the Offie awards for *Br'er Cotton* at Theatre 503 and for *Thebes Land* at the Arcola Theatre. She is a former resident artist at Kenya's Kuona Arts Trust in Nairobi and resident designer for Istanbul's Talimhane Theatre. Her recent UK design credits include: *Hansel and Gretel* (Opera for Hidden Woods, Iford Arts), *Br'er Cotton* (Theatre 503, Nominated for Best Set Design and Winner of Best New Play at the Offie Awards), *The Majority* (Dorfman, National Theatre), *New Nigerians, Thebes Land* (Nominated for Best Set Design and Winner of Best Production in the Offie Awards), *Maria de Buenos Aires* (Arcola), *Parallel Yerma* (Young Vic), *License to Ill, This Will End Badly, Little Malcolm and his struggle against the Eunuchs* (Southwark Playhouse), *Biedermann and the Arsonists, Synergies: NEBT* (Sadlers Wells), *Mapping Brent*

(Tricycle Theatre), *Dyl, Sparks* (Old Red Lion), *Hearing Things* (Albany), *The Dark Room* (Theatre 503), *The Tempest* (Watermill Theatre), *I Love You, You're Perfect, Now Change* (Zorlu Centre, Istanbul). Jemima has also designed events, merchandise and foyers for the National Theatre, King's Cross Theatre and Waldorf Hotel. She has run workshops and worked on community projects for The Young Vic, Kiln Theatre (The Tricycle), Iford Arts and the National Theatre.

Amy Mae (Lighting Designer)
Amy works across theatre, dance, site-specific and devised performance. She won the Knight of Illumination Award in 2016 for the London production of the acclaimed 'Pie Shop' version of *Sweeney Todd: The Demon Barber of Fleet Street*, and her designs for the New York production have been nominated for the 2017 Drama Desk Award for Outstanding Lighting Design and the Lucille Lortel Award for Best Lighting. Upcoming credits include *Wild East* (Young Vic, Genesis Directors Award). Recent Credits include: *Hansel and Gretel* (Rose Theatre, Kingston), *The Fishermen* (Edinburgh Fringe, UK Tour), *Three Sat Under The Banyan* (Polka Theatre), *About Leo* (Jermyn Street), *Mountains: The Dreams of Lily Kwok* (Royal Exchange), *Exploding Circus* (Pavilion Theatre, Worthing), *Br'er Cotton* (Theatre 503), *Othello, Jekyll and Hyde* and *The Host* (NYT Rep Season 2017), *Half Breed* (Talawa/Soho Theatre & Assembly Rooms), *Start Swimming* (Young Vic/Summerhall Edinburgh), *The Ugly One* (Park Theatre), *Babette's Feast* (The Print Room), *The Lounge* (Soho Theatre), *Paradise of the Assassins* (Tara Theatre), *Knife Edge* (Pond Restaurant, Dalston), *Prize Fights* (Royal Academy of Dramatic Art), *Orphans* (Southwark Playhouse), *Macbeth* (Italia Conti), *I'm Not Here Right Now* (Paines Plough Roundabout and Soho Theatre), *Liola* (New Diorama Theatre), *Children in the Uniform, Punk Rock* (Tristan Bates Theatre), *Sweeney Todd* (Harringtons Pie and Mash Shop, West End & Off-Broadway). Amy trained at RADA on the postgraduate Stage Electrics and Lighting Design course and has a degree in Stage Management and Performing Arts from the University of Winchester. She was one of the invited speakers at the 2017 Showlight Conference in Florence.

Odinn Orn Hilmarsson (Sound Designer)
Odinn is an Icelandic composer and sound designer based in London. Using a mixture of traditional instruments and experimental digital processing, he creates textured and unique sounds and compositions. Recently Odinn has contributed to the immersive show *Reflected* (The Milo Wladek Co.), the *Eastenders* podcast (BBC Sounds), *The Zoe Ball Book Club* (ITV & Cactus TV). Previously he and Roy Alexander Weise worked together on the National Youth Theatre's production of *Jekyll & Hyde* in 2017 and together with Eve Leigh on *Stone Face* in 2016.

Thomas Bailey (Assistant Director)
Thomas' directing credits include *Mrs Dalloway* (Arcola), *Callisto: a queer epic* (Arcola), *The Games We Played* (Theatre 503), *Rehearsing for Planet B* (North Wall Arts Centre), *Romeo and Juliet* (Southwark Playhouse & International Tour) and *The Pillowman* (Oxford Playhouse). He is joint Artistic Director of Forward Arena, and worked as NYT Rep Bryan Forbes Assistant Director throughout 2017, during which he assisted Roy Alexander Weise and was mentored by Carrie Cracknell.

Julia Nimmo (Stage Manager)
Julia trained in Design for Theatre & Television at Charles Stuart University, Wagga Wagga, Australia. As a Stage Manager her theatre credits include: *Macbeth* (Wildfire Productions, Cell Block Theatre, Sydney), *The Beauty Queen Of Leenane* (Wildfire Productions, Seymour Centre, Sydney), *The Real Thing* (English Touring Theatre, 2012 UK Tour), *The One* (Soho Theatre), *Beached* (Marlow Theatre & Soho Theatre), *Lampedusa* (HighTide & Soho Theatre), *Flare Path* (Birdsong Productions & Original Theatre, 2016 UK Tour), *This Much* (Moving Dust, Soho Theatre), *Harrogate* (HighTide, Royal Court & UK Tour), *Edward II* (The Marlowe Society & Cambridge Arts Theatre, Cambridge Arts Theatre), *All The Things I Lied About* (Paul Jellis Ltd, Soho Theatre & 2017 UK Tour), *Frankie Vah* (Paul Jellis Ltd, Soho Theatre and 2018 UK tour), *Paper, Scissors, Stone* (Tara Finney Productions, The Vaults Festival 2018 & Live Theatre), *Songlines* (HighTide, Edinburgh Fringe Festival and 2018 UK Tour), *Witches* (Hertfordshire County Youth Theatre, Watford Palace). Festival credits include: *WOW Festival* (Hull 2017), *Talawa First Festival* (2017 & 2018).

Steve Watling (Production Manager)
Steve has over 20 years' experience of working within a variety of areas in theatre & dance performance. Working initially in stage management, then moving in to technical stage management and then on to production management. As a freelance practitioner for over 10 years, Steve has worked as Production Manager with a number of theatre & dance companies, these include a 12-month international tour with 1927's *The Animals & Children Took to the Streets*, national tours of The Paper Birds' *Mobile*, a touring site-specific caravan based show, The West Yorkshire Playhouses' national tour of *Beryl* to theatres & rural venues. Steve has worked as Production Manager on a number of festivals, including Leeds Transform 19 and HighTide Festival Aldeburgh.

Recently Steve took Second Hand Dance's show, *Getting Dressed* on a four-week tour of Sweden and to the International Performing Arts for Youth festival in Philadelphia.

Characters

1, a woman over 65, who plays MIRA.

2, a woman who is much younger.

3, a woman somewhere between their ages.

4, a man over 65, who plays JONAH.

This play should never ask the audience
to believe what is not true.

The story 1 tells is a retelling of "The Little Shoemaker"
by Isaac Bashevis Singer, of blessed memory.

… is an unvoiced response or a euphemism.

/ is an interruption.

– is a sharp cutoff. Or a pivot of thought.

*Ungrammatical commas mark a pivot of thought,
or an effort to convey ideas more clearly.*

*When a line of dialogue begins with a lower case letter, it's because
it's finishing a thought the previous speaker has started.*

A stage, empty apart from a goldfish in a goldfish bowl, on a low bench.

1 enters.

She acknowledges the audience.

She feeds the fish.

She is delighted by its gobbling little face.

She plays with it, a bit.

She scoops it out of the water with her bare hands.

She cradles it in her hands.

She drops it on the floor with a little splash.

We watch it die.

It takes as long as it takes.

It is gasping.

It is dead.

She scoops it off the floor.

She puts it back in the bowl.

She waits for it to move.

It doesn't.

She taps the side of the glass.

Nothing.

Again.

And again nothing.

She taps the side again, peering into the bowl, staring intently at the goldfish.

The goldfish comes back to life. It swims around happily.

It's obviously a toy of some sort.

She grins at the audience.

She inclines her head modestly. She encourages the audience to applaud.

A beat.

1:       I must be honest, I'm not sure I can tell you when it started.

The other actors enter. At first only the women speak.

1:       It could have started with the fire, but that's obviously too late.

2:       Maybe when I started wearing reading glasses, but that's early, that's – that doesn't really feel like when it began.

1:       No, that's, just, reading glasses, that's just a part of life, isn't it?

3:       First grey hairs?

          No, too early.

1:       For me I believe it started when men stopped offering to buy me drinks in public places.

2:       When I started being nervous on the stairs.

3:     When I came out the womb I *started* getting older.

2:     No, no, well, I suppose menopause is an obvious place to start.

3:     When my dad's spunk hit my mum's egg and my first cells started dividing, yeah, that's when it started, ever since I've just been getting older.

1:     When I saw him again after he had been dead for seven months.

2:     When it hurt to get out of bed in the morning, no, too early,

1:     I think it's probably hurt to get out of bed in the morning since I was a teenager, no.

3:     When I started receiving my pension? No, that's stupid.

2:     Free bus fare?

3:     Oh, please be quiet, you're embarrassing me.

1:     Maybe it was when I started to be able to say what I thought and I knew no one would –

2:     not mind –

1:     no, it's not that they wouldn't mind, it's just that they'd think I was… "feisty" or…

2:     Or an arsehole, or…

1:     Yes, an arsehole, but not relevant enough –

3:     not important enough, not meaningful enough

2:       to be rude to.

1:       It was the way people started speaking to me at work. The way they'd be polite to me.

2:       Maybe it was once I had children, maybe that was the beginning.

3:       Maybe it was after the divorce.

2:       Maybe it was once we bought the house and I had to – I'm very lucky obviously, I'm incredibly lucky, but you just start needing to make different decisions once you have a mortgage to keep up, I know it sounds stupid but I think, if I'm honest, yes, you could start there as well as anywhere else.

The only man speaks.

4:       For me –

Everyone waits.

4:       For me it was a conversation I had with,

        a delicate – conversation –

        with this very young, junior doctor,

        who was explaining the decision not to treat my prostate cancer.

        …

        She said it grows very slowly,

        the treatment, is,

        awful, the treatment is really painful,

and often it doesn't work, and the form of cancer you have, the form of prostate cancer

takes decades to kill you.

So…

So what?

So. It – doesn't make sense. To treat it.

Oh.

And I wasn't going to be difficult, or get – *(the missing word is "emotional".)*

Oh. I see.

Yes.

…

Yes, so.

It was then, I think.

A pause.

The women go back to speaking.

1:       When I realised I had to be very, I could no longer,

3:       I couldn't make coffee, while getting dressed, or whatever, I needed to be careful and concentrate while getting dressed because if I didn't I might just leave the house with no trousers on.

2:       It's really not a joke.

3:      Oh but it's funny, it IS funny –

2:      why are they laughing?

3:      Oh God, if we can't laugh about all this we're all fucked,

She seems like she's about to say something more but she doesn't.

4:      *(Filling the awkward space, very proudly.)*
        My bar mitzvah!

2:      When it – maybe –

        No no. I know.

        I know, actually.

        For me it was, I went to, a magic show, we were in Las Vegas all of the girls, and it was, the audience was really into it, like close-up magic, things appearing and disappearing, all that, and everyone seemed so excited, at first I thought ugh these –

        sorry but –

        these stupid Americans, roaring and whooping when you can clearly see he's just picking up a lemon from under that cabinet, he's just used a different dove, he's just –

        but the girls were –

        Everyone was,

        really enjoying it.

        Everyone was fooled.

...

Misdirection, he –

he was telling us all where to look. And where not
to look. Yes?

And everyone was, following him, everyone was –
looking, where he wanted them to look, it's – you
have to do it, you HAVE to, it's just instinct.

But something, in my brain

something was going on –

which meant I wasn't seeing things like everyone
else.

...

I wasn't getting the signal.

Everyone was roaring, roaring.

And that's when I knew.

Oh, God.

Something is really wrong.

3:      Maybe it wasn't when I left the womb, maybe it
        was when I learned to talk, I have no time before
        language, I have no memory of time, maybe really
        if I think about when it started it was learning
        language in the first place, that was when it began,
        time began to move when I learned to speak.

1:      And listen.

2:      It was when I couldn't stop them from moving into my house.

3:      There is a language we never forget, we always know and we never forget, that language, that language is where it begins.

* * *

3:      It's mad. I still don't know how it happened!

MIRA: Oh, me neither, me neither.

3:      Fixed, anyway.

2:      Yeah!

3:      New stove installed, tiling fixed –

MIRA: I – saw –

3:      Fresh – paint, fresh extractor –

MIRA: Yes. Yeah, it looks wonderful, thank you.

2:      And you're comfortable with using the new one?

MIRA: Yes I am.

2:      Because it wouldn't be anything, to

        we could just go through, and make sure

MIRA: Yes I'm, it's not, complicated, yes.

2:      …

3:      So…

MIRA: So, right, erm, here's… here you go.

She writes a cheque and shoves it in their hands.

3:      Oh, thank you, thanks, madam.

2:      Yeah… thank you.

They do not leave.

MIRA: So…

        do you –

        do you,

        want your coats, or –

3:      No, no, actually, we were –

2:      Could we –

3:      Just stay for a cup of tea?

2:      It's cold, and – we were thinking –

MIRA: Course you can, course you can! I'll just –

3:      No you sit down, we can –

MIRA: Course, you/know where, everything is, don't you?

3:      Yes! Yeah.

2:      You rest yourself.

MIRA: I'm – . Thank you.

One of them goes into the kitchen.

3:        Yeah. We, er…

          We wanted to talk to you, actually.

          We didn't want to leave without – talking to you.

MIRA: About what.

3:        About how the fire started.

MIRA: …oh.

          I mean…

3:        Because it's –

          we were –

          concerned,

          about how it started.

MIRA: Well,

          …

3:        Was it,

          did you,

          forget the burner was on,

          or…

MIRA: No no no.

	Honestly,
	you're such nice girls,
	to be worried about a thing like this.
	but it's, not –
3:	Do you have – family about?
MIRA:	I'm sorry, but – I
3:	please don't answer if it's too
MIRA:	no.
	No, I –
	no.
3:	There's a man gets post here.
MIRA:	Yer, yer, he still –
	My husband. Still gets post.
3:	He – passed on?
MIRA:	Seven months ago. Seven months and six days.
3:	Oh you poor thing, you poor – thing, that's no time at all, is it?
MIRA:	It feels like no time. It feels like – no time, as you say.
3:	Because, we were thinking,
	how did the fire start?

MIRA: I, think it must have been, a, faulty connection with
         the gas or

3:       We checked the gas, we checked the – it's, all all
         right, it was fine.

MIRA: Well then I – really don't know.

2 comes in with the tea.

3:       Because we – we don't want to be, too personal.
         But

2:       Your flat is really lovely!

MIRA: Oh – thank you –

3:       You see our –

         you see where we're coming from.

2:       An,

         a lady at your time of life living on her own with no
         family around and there's this kitchen fire –

MIRA: It's really all right. It was only small.

2:       But you can't – you can't tell us how it happened.

MIRA: …

         You're very sweet girls.

         But –

2:       We promise,

         whatever, happened,

3:      Just tell us what you remember.

MIRA: I'm very careful with it.

2:      Careful with what?

MIRA: I'm very,

          I know,

          I have to be careful,

          I'm not,

          I mean you see, I'm not

          I'm, I have no trouble,

          following, conversations or

          and so I know – I need to be careful, with, keeping
          track of the burners, and…

3:      Course. Common sense.

MIRA: Which is why I know it wasn't me.

2:      What do you mean?

MIRA: I walked into the room and the,

          it was,

          on fire,

          but I hadn't used the stove at all that day,

          I'd been out, I'd been at my niece's, and she lives
          in Melton Mowbray, so it's, we,

I come in after a day out,

nothing, nothing,

and then half an hour later I smell smoke.

3:      Could you have, for/gotten –

MIRA: I didn't forget, I didn't forget, the stove just turned on and then I don't even know how the fire caught but there you go, you saw, it did.

And you saw that fire, well you, you saw the, damage,

that was not a fire that was burning all day, definitely not, it was only burning for a short while, definitely,

and I didn't touch the stove, I didn't touch it all day. Not once.

2:      Could you have forgotten?

MIRA: That's never happened. Never.

3:      Never before.

2:      Do you think someone –

do you think there was, someone. Inside the flat with you.

MIRA: I

don't know.

I think there was,

I don't know,

a fault with the stove,

that was, melted away, by the time you started
work on it. Or something.

…

I heard something. I heard – something.

When I came in that day.

3:      Arson,/is –

2:      We should –

        your neighbours, we should,

        if there's any sign of a break in,

        we should report it,

        that could have been so dangerous,

3:      Arson is a very serious thing.

MIRA: There's no need to get the police involved.

3:      If someone is breaking into your home and setting
        fires,

MIRA: No no, really, please – there's no need.

3:      I think,

        the other people in the block would be concerned,
        I think,

MIRA: Please no – there's –

          It's fine now.

2:        Do you think someone broke in?

3:        Did they take anything?

MIRA: …

2:        Do you think someone broke in?

MIRA: …

          I don't know.

          I – don't know.

          It's hard to say.

3:        Do the other people in the block know you had a
          fire in here?

2:        Does your niece know you had a fire?

MIRA: It's none of anyone's business, and I'm sorry but I
          think you'll have to leave now.

They do not move.

3:        I think your neighbours would want to know. That
          you set a fire and didn't know about it.

2:        It was right under their kitchen too, their kitchen
          could/have caught, the

MIRA: I didn't, I didn't, set the fire, I didn't –

3:      Well either that or there's a break in and arson
        which by rights we should report

MIRA: It's – no – it's none of

2:      I think your niece would want to know a thing like
        this. If I was your niece I'd definitely want to know.

3:      I'd want to know for sure, if it was my auntie.

MIRA: …

        What do you want?

3:      …

        What do you mean?

MIRA: What… do you want?

3:      We, want, to make sure you're safe.

2:      We want to make sure you, don't –

MIRA: I've paid you now get out.

3:      This doesn't just concern you, you know.

2:      There are kids in this block.

3:      Kids, could have

MIRA: I asked you what do you want.

3:      We want the cheque. For our work.

MIRA: I gave you the cheque already.

3:      No you didn't.

MIRA: Yes, I –

2:          I could see how you would be confused but you
            didn't give us a cheque, dear, and we've been
            working in here for days now, we really need to be
            paid.

MIRA: …

3:          If you want we could – call up –

MIRA: Stop trying to tell me I didn't give you the cheque I
            gave it you, I did, I did give it to you –

2:          You're confused, dear.

3:          I'm starting to think you're so confused it's not
            right to leave you alone, I'm starting to think we
            should, maybe, call your niece anyway

2:          Or the police.

3:          Social services.

2:          Lots of –

MIRA gets out the chequebook.

She looks at them.

2:          Lots of options.

She writes out another cheque.

3:          Thank you.

2:          Yeah, thanks, it was a lovely job.

3:          You've been lovely.

She says nothing. They go. She hears the door click.

She is shaking.

She moves to clear the mugs.

3:        Sorry –

She jumps.

3:        Sorry.

          I was –

          We've just realised…

          This is awkward.

          You've paid her,

          but you've not paid me.

MIRA: I've paid you the price we agreed.

3:        For her, yes, you paid the price we agreed for one
          person but not for both of us.

MIRA: …

          That is not true, we agreed –

3:        To a price for one person's labour per day. And
          you had two people's labour.

2:        Honestly it would have worked out the same either
          way, I just would have worked twice as long.

MIRA: I've already paid you twice now. I've paid you
          twice what we agreed.

2:      I'm sorry you're not following, dear, but you need
        to pay us the full amount.

MIRA: I've paid you twice and this will be –

3:      Do you want to shout?

        Do you want to get the neighbours, and tell them –

MIRA: The cheque will bounce, I don't have enough in
        my account.

Beat.

3:      Why tell us that, though. If it were true.

        …

        You could have just wrote it and let it bounce, it
        would've gotten us out of your house.

        So basically I don't believe you, I don't actually
        think it would bounce.

MIRA: …Could I give you something. To pay you. Some,
        ah, my television or –

3:      Taking something out of your home?

2:      Not likely.

3:      That would be like stealing.

2:      If the police found it round one of ours, what
        would they think?

3:      We really just want to be paid for the work we've
        done.

2:      We could have just done the stove and left the wall and extractor in a state.

3:      We could have.

2:      If you want we can mess up the wall again, mess up the extractor, so it's a bit like how it would have been if we'd just done the stove.

4 enters, playing JONAH.

MIRA sees him but tries not to let on.

The other two are vaguely aware of something different in the room but can't see him. Maybe they feel a chill that they can't place.

3:      We have the tools.

2:      I mean it hardly compensates us for the time but we can do it if that's how you want it.

JONAH: Try shame.

MIRA: *(To JONAH.)* What?

3:      We're not joking.

JONAH: Try shame. Always worth a shot with young people.

MIRA: *(To 2 and 3.)* Well. That seems very ugly.

3:      Not as ugly as cheating someone out of the salary they need to live.

JONAH: Remember I see them too.

MIRA: Would you really do that?

I'm looking at your hands.

Would you actually just – take a cold chisel to the wall or something, is that something you've done before?

Is that the sort of thing you normally, have you done this a lot?

2:       Don't know what/you're talking about, dear.

JONAH: They want you to pay too much, yes?

MIRA: *(Upset by them talking over each other, trying to keep it together.)* Stop it, I don't –

3:       Who are you talking to?

JONAH: They want you

         to pay *too much.*

MIRA: Of course.

         Of course.

She writes a cheque and drops it to the ground.

A beat.

3 stoops for it.

But MIRA is already writing another cheque. And another.

They hesitate. They do not touch the cheques.

MIRA: Go on then, girls.

         Go on then.

She is filling out the whole chequebook.

JONAH is watching eagerly.

MIRA: I'm forgetting, I'm forgetting every second I wrote
          one oopsie, oooh dear, there's another one I forgot,
          go on and take them girls, nothing suspicious about
          this at all, go right abloodylong, is there anything
          you've forgotten?

2:        …

          I think that –

MIRA: I said is there anything you've forgotten I said.

          Have you forgotten, maybe,

          have you accidentally forgotten and asked me to
          write two cheques for the total, instead of one?

2:        Er…

3:        No. No we haven't.

MIRA: That one thinks you might have forgotten –

3:        No she doesn't, she was just confused, but thank
          you, we are going to go ahead and leave now so –

MIRA: How will I heat the flat.

          How will I cook. For the second half of the month.
          Without the second cheque.

3:        There is no second cheque.

MIRA: Except that when you came in that's exactly what you said. "You've paid her but you've not paid me."

It will be very serious for me. If I can't…

I'm losing weight, since my husband died.

Everything is colder when you're older.

If I can't –

One of them lets the second cheque drop.

2: I think we picked it up by mistake.

3: Yeah, we must have done.

2: You shouldn't leave all of these lying around.

MIRA: I'll burn them on my brand-new stove.

3: We'll be off now.

JONAH: Ooh, safe journey!

MIRA: Safe journey now!

3: Good night.

They go. JONAH gets the giggles. MIRA does too.

JONAH: I don't think I –

I don't think I'll,

go off, anymore.

I think it might work better if I'm just with you all the time.

MIRA: Oh but that wasn't your fault I'm fine to be on my own some of the time that was just –

JONAH: I just think it'd be

lovely

if I'm here all the time.

MIRA: …

(Beaming.) We-ell –

* * *

A burst of tropical music – something joyful, sexy, sounding a bit like the 60s, brilliant to dance to. Maybe 'O Canto A Ema' or 'Chiclete Com Banana' by Gilberto Gil, or 'Soy Loco Por Ti America' by Caetano Veloso. JONAH and MIRA dance together.

The music fades down, but they keep dancing.

2:         Magic is what goes against the laws of nature.

Magic is what makes us feel we know less than we think.

MIRA: I always wanted to go back to Dominica again! Maybe we can, now?

3:          It's the conflict between your automatic mind and the fresh information coming in.

JONAH: Sure, baby, why not?

MIRA leaves to make tea.

2:          It's the conflict between what you think is possible and your experience.

So JONAH is left alone onstage.

3:          What is vision?

2:          A forced agreement between the worlds we see in each eye.

JONAH is watching 2 and 3. And the audience.

3:          There's a tenth of a second processing delay in our vision –

3:          – which means our brains are estimating what the world is likely to be right now.

JONAH abruptly starts dancing on his own.

2:          So what we see is literally not real. Everything we see is a prediction of the future.

3:          Your visual but not your motor cortex are fooled by illusions. *(As she throws something at the nearest audience member.)* Here, catch this.

2:          We don't see what we don't expect.

3:          We think we're moving through the world, in this way, for these reasons, but really –

MIRA enters, cup of tea in hand. She sits by the goldfish.

2:          …

JONAH sits by MIRA. He rests his hand alongside hers.

3:          So,

            if we're tricked,

            it means our brains are working the way they're
            supposed to.

            We're very good at processing what we need. To
            keep moving.

She looks at his hand.

She looks at him.

She takes a sip of tea, smiling.

* * *

JONAH and MIRA are looking at the goldfish. A beat.

MIRA: Does she look fat to you?

JONAH: …

            I don't know

            what a fat goldfish looks like.

27

A beat.

MIRA: It might not be a problem at all.

JONAH: No, it might be fine.

MIRA: They will just keep eating is the thing.

JONAH: I know, that's why I was always the one to feed her.

        And the tank, the tank as well. There's got to be a better way.

MIRA: There isn't, I've tried.

JONAH: But look at her!

MIRA: I can't carry it on my own, it's too heavy.

JONAH: Erm… could you do it in mugs?

MIRA: What do you mean?

JONAH: Just – sink a mug into the tank, and drag it out, and dump it in the sink, and fill it up again, and dump it in, and boom boom boom, do that a few times, the water's – pretty clean!

MIRA: That's exactly what I'm doing now.

JONAH: That's what you're doing now?

MIRA: That's what I'm doing now.

JONAH: Well it isn't good enough.

MIRA: Look at it, it doesn't look bad.

JONAH: It looks different, and not in a good way.

MIRA: You can't even see a difference, you're just being
           stubborn –

JONAH: It is different, I can tell it's different, I know it's
           different, look at her, she's different.

MIRA: Stubborn as the day you were born…

JONAH: She doesn't like it. She can feel the difference and
           she doesn't like it.

MIRA: How can you tell?

JONAH: Because

           …

           I can talk to animals now.

MIRA: …?

JONAH: Yes. Yes I can. And she needs fresher water, that's
           what she's telling me.

MIRA: You cannot. You cannot talk to animals.

JONAH: Yes I can.

MIRA: Prove it.

JONAH: She thinks… you look pretty today.

           She likes it when you smile.

           And you should change her water more.

MIRA: Those don't really sound like thoughts that a fish
           would have.

JONAH: She's having them, I'm telling you right now she's having them, she's just swimming around being a bit hungry and needing a change of water and being happy cause she can see your face.

MIRA: OK what's she thinking right now?

JONAH: Is it possible that you're jealous because you don't get to have the same in-depth conversations with the fish that I do?

MIRA: We're going to test this.

JONAH: Fine, fine.

MIRA: I'm going to put my finger up to the bowl and she will not come gobbling at it like I have food, you will tell her not to, she will just relax, she will ignore me.

She does it. The goldfish ignores her...

JONAH: Ha! Ha, see?

... until she notices her finger and starts gobbling at it.

MIRA: A ha, a ha, what do you call that?

JONAH: Goldfish have short memories, I can't be responsible for all that, I told her.

MIRA: How does it work, then. How does it work that you talk to animals.

JONAH: It's you know, I'm on a plane.

A different plane.

I hear many voices.

MIRA: Right, what's the wall saying then?

JONAH: The wall

          is a bit stiff.

MIRA: Admit that you are lying you liar and we can put
          this all behind us.

JONAH: We can't put this behind us because

          we need a better system for the fish.

          Don't overfeed her, don't starve her, and don't kill
          her with some nasty tank juice.

MIRA: Simple enough, right?

JONAH: Simple enough.

MIRA: I've always had this problem, you remember, I've
          never been able to with the routine things, the,
          routines, they've never

JONAH: You're a philosopher, you need to concern yourself
          with… philosophical things, that's why we're so
          good together.

MIRA: I should be the one that talks to animals.

JONAH: Well what if it was every day? Every day you
          change the water a little bit?

MIRA: They get upset if you do that.

JONAH: The fish gets upset? Look who talks to animals
          now.

MIRA: I can't lift it.

I'm telling you.

I can't lift it on my own.

JONAH: Mondays, Wednesdays, Fridays, changing it.

You know which day it is, right?

MIRA: I can always check.

JONAH: Food, can you peg it to your meals?

MIRA: I don't eat at regular times. I don't eat a – regular, number of meals.

JONAH: …

MIRA: It, I don't like it, I – I get full so easily.

JONAH: Not even a bit of ice cream?

MIRA: *(Smiling.)* I – it's just – I just –

JONAH: You need to try.

MIRA: It – I – really –

JONAH: You – please, you need to try, if you got ill or if – something else went wrong, you need to be – nutrition is important.

MIRA: …

JONAH: What?

MIRA: … "nutrition is important."

JONAH: Mira –

MIRA: Leave me, let me – please don't –

JONAH: I love you.

MIRA: Don't tell me what's important, NOTHING – I'm

                trying to –

JONAH: I really think –

                                    *   *   *

1, alone.

1:           There was once a shoemaker that everyone called
             the little shoemaker because he was little but
             powerful,

             you know, sort of built like a barrel,

             but very small.

             He was from a long line of shoemakers who were
             short but powerful, and for generations they would
             sit together

             Brothers and fathers and grandfathers together,

             making shoes on this long low bench by the fire.

             And what happened is the little shoemaker had
             fourteen strong sons and he was very lucky,
             obviously, but what happened is one by one they

left to seek their fortune in America. And they wrote to him like good sons, and they always sent money for the synagogue back home, but they were always saying to the little shoemaker that he should follow them to America, that where he was there was no future.

But the shoemaker always refused. He didn't want to go to America, and anyway who would look after the graves of his mother and father if he was to leave? He couldn't bear the shame of them having overgrown graves. He couldn't even bear the thought of it.

And soon enough the war came, and his sons said, are you mad, war will be coming to our village soon and you're an old man now, you will be helpless, you will die a terrible death, you must come to America.

But no. He was stricken with the same terrible thought of his parents, who had cared for him, loved him, given him life, his parents' names disappearing, the graves overcome with weeds. There was no one left to take care of them. He would not go.

And then, as his sons had predicted – war came to the village, the bombs came down screaming, but it was only when the synagogue roof itself caught fire that the little shoemaker consented to be evacuated.

And when he was in America, my God. It had been forty years since he'd seen his oldest boy. He wouldn't have recognised him if he hadn't known. He was so American. Bragging all the time as if he'd done something, when all he'd done is, probably he would die richer than he was born. So? Is that a thing to be so puffed up about?

And his grandchildren! Loud, running around, disrespecting their parents, didn't speak even one word of Yiddish. And so the little shoemaker could not communicate with them.

The first day he got there, he sat down with his tools by the fire. But his sons explained that people didn't have handmade shoes in America, and anyway he was old, he should relax and enjoy himself!

But that is not what happened.

What happened is the little shoemaker disappeared.

He went to sleep when he was told, and got up when he was told, and ate when he was told, but otherwise there was nothing of him left. First the hours lost their shape, then the days. Then the rooms of the house lost their shape and he could no longer distinguish between the walls and the doors, the ceiling and the floors. And everything was unknitted from itself.

Until one day. He saw a familiar shape.

And he asked himself, what is that shape?

Why do I know it?

And then he realised: it was his sack of tools from his lost village.

He had forgotten everything.

But his hands still remembered.

And he sat by the fire with the scraps of leather still in his bag and he made a shoe,

such a small shoe,

a small and perfect shoe such as they always made in his village, such as the men of his family had always, always made.

And his grandchildren saw it, how what was flat was given shape so quickly, so skilfully, and they tried to discover the trick in his hands. Because what he was doing was obviously magic.

And he gestured to his grandchildren – because they had no words for each other, but you don't need words for this, you can't teach people to make things with words, they need to feel them coming into being under their fingers.

And when the son came home that day he saw on a long low bench by the fire a row of little shoemakers, making magic, led by the last,

the very last of his kind.

* * *

MIRA and JONAH visit a MEDIUM, played by 3.

3:        Very strong, yes?

          Very strong.

          Now what are you telling me, my angels.

          My angels are saying you've mellowed a lot,
          actually, they're saying you used to be very – fiery,
          very strong sense of what's right and what's not
          right, the right way to treat people. Very strong
          sense of how you want to be treated.

MIRA recognises herself, sheepishly. JONAH chuckles in spite of himself.

3:        It's very attractive, it's a very attractive quality, I
          think you are a magnetic person, you really draw –
          people, and energy, to yourself.

          But as you've gotten older, and it's not a good thing
          and it's not a bad thing, you're able to let things
          lie a little bit more. It can go either way, as you get
          older, some people get very angry, but I think for
          you you're sort of more able to allow people to be
          who they are and – just let them be, who they are.

          That's right, isn't it?

MIRA: That's... yes, I – know what you mean, yes.

3:        No I can tell, I can tell, something about – I can
          see.

          Now what are you telling me, my angels.

My angels are telling me that they want to see your palms, yes, they want to have a look at them palm side up –

yes, brilliant –

and now hand side up, like back of the – perfect.

Hmm.

My angels are saying you're very – nurturing – yes, like you're very,

you're a very caring person, very giving, you really enjoy looking after things.

JONAH: Dunno what the goldfish would say about that…

MIRA: *(Directed at JONAH.)* The angels are obviously very nice people.

3:     Now what are you telling me, my angels.

MIRA: Listen, I – not to interrupt the, angels, but –

3:     Yes?

MIRA: – I just have a question.

         …

The way you described me, it – erm – made sense to me, and I think it would make sense, to,

people who know me, people who've known me for a long time –

JONAH snorts.

MIRA: But honestly,

          not to, I don't want to, be –

          but you could have said I was a real pushover, and
          I could probably think of loads of times when I
          should have stood up for myself and didn't, and I
          would have recognised myself, just the same. And
          you would have said exactly the opposite thing.

          So I suppose I wonder –

          how do you do this?

          How do you keep doing this do you feel, that you
          have a mission, or

          do you really hear voices and "the angels" are
          making you, or

3:        That's a good question, that's a very important
          question.

          Hmm.

          Well, you know, it makes no difference to me really
          whether you believe me or not. It's not important
          to me at all.

MIRA: Really?

3:        Really, yes, I hope I can be useful, but your beliefs
          are your own business.

          And people usually come here, it's my experience,
          when their old beliefs are not serving them very
          well.

But your beliefs are your beliefs and I really don't
know.

MIRA makes a noise to indicate that the MEDIUM should continue.

3:    And you're right – I could direct your attention to,
two, contradictory things about yourself, and they
would both be right. Because human beings are
complicated, and life is complicated. Right?

But, my God. Imagine second-guessing every little
thing you noticed about yourself or other people,
you'd die of exhaustion, it'd just be so boring.
And pointless! You get by well with the first things
you've noticed, that's just how we're built, we've
survived the way we have because our instincts are
usually trustworthy.

So, that means – looking where we're inclined to
look. Listening to the angels. And moving forward,
on that basis, which is really –

MIRA: – yes –

3:    Limited, and –

MIRA: yes.

3:    Is that all right for you, would you like to continue?

MIRA avoids JONAH's eye. She nods.

3:    OK. So.

My angels are saying you're moving into a time of
uncertainty, that right now everything is confused,
you had a shock,

yes, a serious shock, very serious,

hmm, it feels like it was yesterday,

but it wasn't yesterday, was it, it just feels like,

it always feels like it just happened.

JONAH looks at MIRA, and is quiet.

MIRA: … yes.

3:            You have come here today to find out how to get
              over this shock, yes?

MIRA: No. That's not why I've come here.

3:            Why have you come here?

MIRA: …

              I have the time.

              I thought it'd be… if I'm honest…

              (Looks at JONAH.)

              I don't know.

3:            Sometimes the spirits have a funny way of bringing
              you to them. Even if you don't exactly know why.

MIRA: I do know, *why* – I just don't want to tell you.

3:            Why don't you want to tell me?

MIRA: It's – not polite.

3:            The truth is always better.

MIRA: I thought it'd be funny.

           (JONAH gives her a look.)

3:         …

           well.

           Maybe it is funny.

           Laughing would be good for you right now, that's
           what my angels are saying.

MIRA: Would you be able to sense a – presence, a spiritual
           presence in this room?

3:         I believe so, yes.

*JONAH starts doing a silly dance around the room. MIRA tries not to
laugh.*

3:         I sense,

           well let me be careful what I say here,

           since this shock, that you had – yesterday and not
           yesterday,

           …

           it's very difficult –

           no, let me start over.

           When we're young,

           if we have a shock,

           if we – fall down a flight of stairs, or,

yes, yes if we fall down a flight of stairs,

a seven-year-old will not injure themselves as badly on the stairs as a forty-seven-year-old. Or a seventy-seven-year-old.

And this is for many reasons, our bodies are more resilient in – many, many different ways, when we're young.

But shock. Shock and fear.

(JONAH is still.)

Is different in the bodies of the old than the bodies of the young.

People are changed by the shocks they get in their old age, and it is completely unrealistic to expect that they will go back the way they were before.

So when I say to you that I sense a dark presence around you, a dark spirit, that came to you after that shock –

(JONAH is horrified.)

Understand I don't, this isn't, wrraaagh, *The Exorcist*, it's not,

I don't mean like a different, maybe not a different, spirit, but something was released,

and I don't want to scare you,

but it is blocking your light *(JONAH moves toward MIRA. MIRA is taking all of this in.)* and it is keeping you from getting better.

MIRA: I'm sorry but you don't know what you're talking
           about.

3:         I know it's difficult to hear but –

MIRA: What language do the angels speak?

           Do they speak Hebrew, or,

           Ancient Greek,

           did you just think there was

           babble in your head

           and then you started studying Biblical Hebrew by
           MASSIVE COINCIDENCE, and all of a sudden –

3:         The angels,

           they don't speak in a, language language,

           it's more of a knowing.

MIRA: Ah. A knowing.

           I couldn't keep a cactus alive, nurturing and
           caretaking, I think you should admit that you saw
           I'm an old woman and you're making your best
           guesses here.

JONAH: Mira, please don't –

3:         You're right, I'm doing my best and, I, all I can do
           is, my best. But if you have such a strong reaction
           to –

MIRA: I'm having a strong reaction because you're wrong, you're wrong and you're – irresponsible, going round mucking in other people's lives.

JONAH: Mira, she's not –

MIRA: *(To JONAH.)* Don't defend her!

3:       *(Noticing that MIRA has spoken to thin air.)* I'm sorry I've upset you, madam. I really didn't mean to.

MIRA: You haven't upset me, you're just talking nonsense about very personal things that's not you upsetting me, that's you,

         doing

         a very upsetting thing.

3:       It's not good to see a medium within the first year of a bereavement. It brings up too much.

MIRA: … I know you're just guessing but that's a horrible thing to, guess about, that's horrible…

3 stands up and indicates that MIRA should go.

3:       Well maybe I made a mistake, madam. Only you would know. Have a nice day.

MIRA and JONAH are suddenly outside. The sound of a high wind.

MIRA: I think I'm going to have, tuna for lunch today, I think I'm gonna fix myself a nice tuna sandwich/ and

JONAH: Mira.

MIRA: I'm going to have, toast probably, what?

JONAH: …

MIRA: No.

No, no, she was,

a fraud, she was a total, she was wrong, you

JONAH: you're right, you're right, what did she know, she
how could she

no, but,

no, but,

you, how will you take care of yourself if I leave,
what if there's a, or what if, will you just watch
telly,

You can't, I can't leave, I

MIRA: You can't, you can't.

JONAH: …

but

…

if I were to, maybe only breakfast, maybe just at
the beginning of the day, if I could just be there at
the beginning, or would you

no

would you live for the beginning of the day, would
it just make everything else…

would you?

MIRA: *(Lying.)* No, no,

            I could… just see you in the morning and then, go about my day or,

JONAH: You could?

MIRA: Probably.

JONAH: …

            It would just be…

            all –

            right?

            If I wasn't there?

MIRA: …I

            I

            whatever I have to do

            if it's only in the mornings I would wake up for breakfast! Probably! It would be easy to remember when to feed the fish if it was only –

JONAH: Would it be all right. If I was gone. Would it, not, would you –

MIRA: …

            this is a terrible, Jonah, you are putting me in a terrible position, because if I say it'll be fine you'll go and if I tell the truth that I have no idea, I have no idea how anyone would keep going with so little to love in the world, that of course –

of course –

did you not see it, did you not see that yes of COURSE you take me away from the world and who cares, maybe you always took me away from the world, but you're

you're the best reason I know to wake up.

Why would that change?

JONAH: *(Desperate.)* Oh,

oh,

Mira –

JONAH is disappearing. The wind is louder and louder.

MIRA: No no no it'll do no good you'll go for no reason, how will that, help, I can't leave you! I can't – *leave!* – I will die! You have to stop, you have to stop, you have to –

JONAH is gone – he has disappeared back into the chorus.

MIRA does not believe it.

MIRA: Oh –

oh –

The wind dies. Maybe she's inside now. Anyway, it's quiet.

MIRA: I've never believed in, any,

afterlife,

but I knew – I KNEW! – I'd see you again. It didn't surprise me, didn't surprise me at all. So you know.

And – so you know – I – didn't understood, I understood nothing, when I was young, I didn't know how to feel, I didn't know how to – taste, it is such a blessing to get old, it's a blessing to have time.

And you know, I do feel it, life is still so good, and I'm in pain but life is still so good, but I see a green pepper and I think about how you hate green pepper and I – *remember* –

how can I be bothered to keep – cooking if you go,

such a mess,

and then clearing up, how can I be bothered, how can I keep on making a mess and clearing it up and making a mess and – clearing it up –

if it's not for, anyone, or anything I love –

…

I still love the world. I still love the world.

Please don't leave.

But JONAH is gone forever.

MIRA crumbles into herself.

She sits down,

and we see the character disappear.

The actor playing MIRA is empty.

* * *

The only actor who wasn't directly involved in the last scene speaks to the audience:

2:          OK. We need a volunteer.

There is (probably) a long pause. The actors should be patient. They may ad lib to get people onstage, but only from a position of total comfort with nothing happening onstage for a bit.

In other words, it should be the audience's discomfort that propels one of them onstage.

When the volunteer enters, she/he is welcomed by the performers.

2:          Thanks so much for joining us, what's your name?

The volunteer gives her/his name.

2:          [Name], what a beautiful name. Have a seat!

The volunteer sits.

2:          Could you just – have a look at this waiver –

The waiver says:

"This is completely scripted.

It is exactly the same every night.

It's absolutely nothing to do with you.

Thanks so much for playing along."

2:          You understand this?

The volunteer indicates that she/he does.

2:          Could you sign it, please?

The volunteer signs.

2:          Thank you, and that's yours to keep.

Now. *(Takes the volunteer's hands, and examines the palms. Throughout the reading, the PALM READER should indicate the particular line or mound on the hand she's referring to. Especially during the very specific predictions.)* It's time for the segment we call, Predict The Audience's Future! *(Wait for/demand applause.)*

So I can see you're a very, a very, adventurous person, yeah, very adventurous.

Looks at hand.

And I think that gets you into trouble sometimes! But I do think that's the best way to be, yeah, I think that's how all the best things in life happen, by going out on a limb. Isn't it?

Looks at hand.

Now this is – this is really unusual. I'm looking at how you spend your time. This is really amazing.

Referring to her/his hand throughout.

It says here that you save the world.

I don't know how, whether it's, are you like a scientist or – *[They're probably not a scientist]* well definitely, I can't actually tell you how but it's in your palm, yeah you're gonna knock climate change on the head most likely, you save the world.

[But if they are a scientist.] Oh yeah, with sciencey stuff probably, yeah you're gonna knock climate change on the head most likely, you save the world.

Looks at hand.

Look at this! This is your true love line, it's very well-defined, you're definitely going to experience true love. And this is your "everyone accepts me" line, and your "no bad things ever happen" line. This is a blessed hand, I'm telling you, we all just want to know it's all gonna be all right, and for [name], it will be!

Looks at hand.

And it seems like after the Revolution you'll live in an anarcho-syndicalist commune with some very nice people and that'll be very satisfying.

Looks at hand.

And so will your kids. Or, not kids, *[Check to see if the volunteer has kids. If so, say:]* "Yes! Your kids! Your kids." *[If not:]* "not – maybe not your *biological* children, it's actually really hard to tell from your palm, but younger people who you love, and who love you, and you look after each other.".)*

Looks at hand.

And… you will die.

There is a pause as she looks at the hand. It should feel possible to the audience that something terrible is about to happen.

And your death will be,

(Beat.)

instant,

and painless,

And then, somehow, you won't be dead?

Could we please get a round of applause for [name.], [he/she] has way less to worry about than the rest of us, and that is well worth celebrating!

The actor and volunteer stand up together. The actor holds the volunteer's hand above her/his head like a champion.

The volunteer returns to her/his seat.

* * *

One of the performers gives a deep, rattling breath.

It is improbably long. It may seem a bit funny.

Then, an improbably long silence. We may worry that it is her last breath.

She exhales. For an improbably long time.

She is silent. And again, we may worry that it is her last breath.

But it is not. Another long, agonisingly laboured intake of breath.

Another performer begins another long painful breath, a few seconds afterward.

They breathe, out of sync with each other, and each breath sounds as if it might be a mercy if it were the last.

MIRA reappears, in the acute care unit of a hospital. It's quite busy and noisy with various monitors and conversations and people coming in and out. A junior doctor and consultant are nearby, discussing her case. Their dialogue swims out of the soundscape of the hospital.

2:          Malnutrition. Hadn't eaten for days, poor thing.

3:          Awful.

2:          Really dehydrated too.

3:          Shouldn't be left on her own, really, it's heartless.

2:          Sometimes it's just not possible to –

3:          *(A bit too loudly.)* Hello. Hello. Are you awake now?

2:          *(A bit too loudly.)* Lucky thing those builders found you, said they wanted to check if the new stove was working, isn't that sweet?

3:	You've had a rough few days, haven't you?
2:	You've been having a rough old time. Not eating, is it?
3:	You're on IV nutrition now, so you should be feeling a bit more hy/drated –
2:	A bit *better*, in a bit.
3:	*(Directed at 2, and not MIRA.)* Someone's brought her food, she can't possibly feed herself yet.

MIRA looks to one side. A tray appears, with a dish of ice cream on it.

2:	*(Directed at 3, and not MIRA.)* I'll get someone to take it away.
3:	Don't you worry about this tray, dear, you're not ready for this quite yet.

They leave.

MIRA looks at the ice cream. A beat.

She knows she is stronger than the doctors realise.

Her breathing is laboured.

She lifts an arm.

She eats a spoonful of the ice cream.

The hospital noise fades.

It tastes so much more like ice cream than she was expecting.

She feels it releasing, unravelling, its coolness, its sweetness.

She swallows.

It's wonderful.

She is eating ice cream as 4 talks.

4:        The trick is – staying vertical.

        Because if they get you horizontal, after a certain point, it's really hard to stand up again.

        …

        So. Pneumonia in one lung.

        Then the blood.

        Then the bladder.

        Then the kidneys.

        Then both lungs.

        She is billowing out in – strange directions these days, glittering spindles of antibiotics and morphine are in her veins, getting fed through a stream in her nose, everyone on the ward is rooting for her to wee, these extraordinary machines bearing her up,

        carrying her forward, just a little further on,

        She is standing on a high bridge, it's not now, it's 1968, she is wearing a pink coat, the sun is at her back.

        An oxygen tank, fire in the blood,

        she longs for the goldfish, she would love to see any living thing that isn't human.

Even the bed rises to meet her,

forward, forward,

every tick of the clock bathed in light.

There is suddenly a drone in the room. 4 can be heard clearly, but is having to work for it a bit.

4:     Fire in the throat,

dying to swallow,

to sit up,

to blink,

to open the eyes,

to moisten the mouth.

The trick, is thinking our bodies can fall apart but, in some, dignified way, the trick is thinking there are some circumstances under which we don't want to live anymore, when we see again and again, at the end we want *LIFE – LIFE – LIFE – LIFE – LIFE!* Just – more – and more – !

The trick is

one minute we're here

and the next –

The tone becomes much more insistent. A beat of suspension.

Four tubs of ice cream with four spoons appear upstage, as if by magic.

All four of the actors take up the tubs and spoons. They eat the ice cream as quickly as possible,

as if something were chasing them,

as if they absolutely must finish before the thing pursuing them catches up.

They push their bodies to the utmost, and it is no trick.

This continues for perhaps two minutes of stage time.

If they get brain freeze or feel sick or just need to pause for breath, it is fully shared with the audience.

The escalation of the tone cues them to fight harder to ram more and more ice cream down.

The cue for them to stop is silence.

* * *

The actors look at the audience. With the sense of shouldering an ancient and burdensome tradition:

4:      We're gonna scatter you someplace you never liked but you went all the time because the kids liked it.

3:      We're gonna not realise what we did to you, we're gonna be really drunk, we're gonna drive away and leave you bleeding, your spouse will never know who killed you.

2:     We're gonna dose you with just the right amount
       of morphine in the last days, when you open your
       eyes which you mostly won't and if you do we'll up
       the morphine but when you do open your eyes

       you will see out the window a beautiful,

       springtime,

       a beautiful springtime

       in the city that you love.

3:     We're gonna resist the urge to shit in your coffin.
       We're gonna hold Gran up as she staggers away
       from the grave.

1:     We're gonna scatter you in the Hudson River.
       And the only thing we'll know for sure about what
       happens next is that the Hudson River goes to
       some very interesting places.

4:     We're gonna play "Always Look On The Bright
       Side Of Life."

2:     We're gonna play "Somewhere Over The
       Rainbow."

1:     We'll sing Jerusalem, just like you had your
       students sing at the end of every school year.

2:     It'll mostly be your students there anyway.

3:     We will celebrate your death as we did your life, by
       mostly talking about ourselves.

4:     We're not gonna pick up the message so we won't
       get to you in time.

3:       We will remember you all our lives and it still won't be enough.

2:       We will share an affectionate memory of you shouting at us over something relatively minor until we pissed ourselves with fear,

3:       and people will think, that is a fairly troubling story to share at a wake, wow.

1:       It will never be enough.

2:       We will try and tell our children everything about you so they will remember you too, sort of, but we won't realise our minds are playing tricks on us,

3:       we will diminish the most magnificent things about you for our own reasons, we will forget the bad because we think it's a service to your memory but it's not, we will forget who you are, we will love you very badly, we will be like those little baby monkeys in that experiment who bonded with a wire dummy with a ticking clock for a heart.

4:       We will remember the heroic fucking things that you did.

1:       And that you hated swearing.

2:       We will remember the look of your hands, and the feel of your hands,

3:       yes, and how the look of your hands changed but the feeling never did.

1:       We will carry your house keys with us everywhere we go.

4:     We will remember the bed,

1:     yes,

4:     there is no bed as empty as the bed

1:     after they take your body away.

2:     When we walk home,

3:     in the frozen dawn,

4:     every street sign we see will feel like a message
       from the universe.

1:     One way.

2:     Floods!

3:     Blind summit.

4:     Stop!

Beat.

1:     Give way.

Small silence.

2:     We will bury you in frozen earth.

       But not yet.

WWW.OBERONBOOKS.COM